SUNSET...
a macular journey

by
Roy Garrabrant

Forward by:
Ronald W. Kristan, MD FACS

authorHOUSE®

AuthorHouse™
1663 Liberty Drive, Suite 200
Bloomington, IN 47403
www.authorhouse.com
Phone: 1-800-839-8640

First published by AuthorHouse 2/21/2008

ISBN: 978-1-4343-5848-6 (sc)

Library of Congress Control Number: 2007909987

Printed in the United States of America
Bloomington, Indiana

This book is printed on acid-free paper.

FORWARD

It is with pleasure and sadness that I write the introduction to this book. And I am honored to have been asked to write it.

I first met Mr. Leroy Garrabrant when he was referred to me by his physician after he had complained of an unusual occurrence in his vision. He indicated to me that he had never had any vision problems except for a few floaters. He was then seventy-one years of age.

After my examination I diagnosed him with early age related macular degeneraton or ARMD for short. Unfortunately this would be the beginning of a long and devastating road to his present condition of severe loss of vision. His ARMD was to be of the most severe and progressive variety despite laser treatment after laser treatment. His chronicle depicts the frustrations we ophthalmologists have in treating this eye condition.

In this book, Mr. Garrabrant describes his odyssey with this devastating disease—and most of it written with very poor vision. He is an inspiration to all with ARMD and certainly to me. Just when he was ready to enjoy his "golden years" his vision was taken from him. And yet as more and more of us live longer we are only going to see ARMD increase dramatically in how many are afflicted.

I thank Mr. Garrabrant immensely for personalizing his ordeal. His story truly touched me and I deal with this condition every day in my practice. He is a brave man and we can all learn from his book—I know I did. Fortunately we are starting to see a lot of research in this field with some new and promising results. Patients like Mr. Garrabrant blazed the trail by telling their story. For all of our future patients with ARMD I am encouraged that their ending will be different.

Ronald W. Kristan, MD FACS

PREFACE

Millions of Americans suffer from loss of vision from Macular Degeneration. The term appears more and more in advertising of various aids for impaired vision. It afflicts the elderly, and is of great concern to them as they face their lives of more dependency.

When I reached age seventy-one I began my struggle with the disease, and in my case it was an unusually long one. I had the opportunity to learn and experience a great deal during the years of treatment and slow descent toward blindness. Over the twelve-year period I had eight doctors who dealt in one way or another with my eye problems. They all were important to me, and from them I gained knowledge, encouragement, and confidence.

I am a mechanical engineer by training, and after a short engineering career, a life in Real Estate. Obviously I write as a patient and report on technical terminology only as I saw it. All that I attempt to do here is describe the social, personal, and emotional sides of my experience. It is my hope that this will be helpful to those who are patients, and those who care for them.

MAINE

Little did I know when I left for my favorite vacation spot that it would also be the beginning of the most fateful journey of my life. The day was perfect. For the past thirty years of our forty-four years of marriage, Del and I vacationed at Kennebunkport, Maine for at least one week in the spring and sometimes for an additional week in the fall. The Port, as we called it, was an historic former shipbuilding center in the eighteenth and nineteenth centuries. The village borders the Kennebunk River and was the site of many Colonial, Georgian and Federal style homes, many having been built and occupied by ship captains. The southeast border of the village is the rockbound coast of the Atlantic Ocean. It became famous in the eighties as the summer home of the forty-first president of the United States. In short, Kennebunkport is a delightful place for rest and relaxation.

It was the fall of nineteen ninety-two, I was seventy-one and had been retired for four years. Del and I were both in excellent health and enjoying our freedom. We spent this day walking along the shore, climbing rocks, and enjoying the scenery. It had been one of those crystal clear days along the Maine coast, the kind when the dark blue ocean meets the slightly paler blue sky at a sharp horizontal line. That evening after dinner at one of our favorite restaurants, we returned to our room and prepared for bed. When my wife Del came out of the bathroom I mentioned that while she was out of the room I had seen a bright light in one of my eyes. She asked if it was flashing and I said that it was more like a searchlight. It was not mentioned again.

After two more days of antiqueing, shopping and generally enjoying the area it was time to go home. The drive of less than four-hundred miles to our North Jersey Shore home was quite easy because we shared the driving. We changed drivers each hundred miles or two hours whichever came first. This arrangement made the trip easier, especially since the Interstates and toll roads we took passed through several heavy traffic areas. The day after our arrival at home, Del said that she wanted me to see my doctor and tell him about the lights in my eyes. She had heard that flashing lights might be an indication of possible stroke susceptibility. I, of course, resisted but knew, after nearly forty years of marriage the easy thing was to see the doctor. He was an internist, and had conducted my annual physicals for several years. My health had been excellent and except for a few minor incidents like sore throats, I had little medical treatment. Even though I saw him a little more than once a year, we had a good relationship and I felt confident in his care and concern. I got an appointment and then it began. After hearing my story the doctor asked if I had an eye doctor. I said that I had had eye exams but was not happy with the doctor and he asked my permission to call and ophthalmologist downstairs. An ophthalmologist is a medical doctor who specializes in treatment and surgery of eyes. He made a call and even though this eye doctor was one of those with a couple of months wait for an appointment, he saw me immediately. He was a nice young man, about the age of my sons. He was thorough, seemed concerned, explained things about my condition, and I liked him. My eyes were dilated and after a short wait for the drops to take effect, and a short question period, he told me that I had such a severe floater problem that he really couldn't see my retina, the light sensitive back of the eye, clearly and would refer me to a retinologist with the necessary equipment for a proper examination. Floaters are the black spots that most of us notice moving around in our eyes. A retinologist is an ophthalmologist who narrows his specialty to the retina part of the eye. A call from the ophthalmologist's assistant got me an appointment the next day with this specialist who also is in high demand with a long waiting time for an appointment. I was beginning to become slightly alarmed. And I had not wanted to start this in the first place.

The new doctor's office was nearby and the following day Del and I drove to his office. I had been warned to have a driver since it wouldn't be safe to drive after the exam. On entering the building we saw the sign which said "Retina Consultants – Practice Limited to Diseases of the Retina." Pretty serious stuff, I thought. This doctor too was old enough to be experienced and young enough to be sharp, and also young enough to outlive me, which gets to be a consideration as we age.

After a pleasant get acquainted period he described a fluoroscene exam that would determine my condition. I think it is called fluoroscopy, and produces photographs of the retina. A special dye is injected into your arm and almost instantly reaches your eye. A series of flash photos show the blood vessels in the retina. Any newly grown vessels are trouble. At this stage of the technology the camera was a Polaroid type, mounted to shoot through the same kind of microscope used for regular eye exams. Ten years later, the photos were all digital and showed up on a computer screen immediately.

Perhaps it was because things were happening so fast, but I don't remember anyone mentioning Macular Degeneration.

Whatever it was, the doctor told me that he wanted me to come in a couple of days later for a laser treatment. That really got my attention. My only knowledge of a laser was that it was a light beam capable of cutting steel, and they were talking about pointing one into one of my eyes and firing it. I remember also that during his explanation, the retinologist, who I would come to admire and trust greatly, said that I was one of the lucky ones. I am still not sure why he said that, but more and more I think it referred to the events which brought me to diagnosis and treatment so fast, beginning with Del's sending me off to the doctor and each of the doctors prompt actions.

The next day, I called the Ophthalmologist and said that the retina man wanted to use a laser and asked if I should let him. His reply was that I should. I did. On that memorable occasion another angiogram was done followed immediately by the laser. The laser is mounted in a regular looking eye-doctors microscope, and at that time gave off bright flashes and loud pops, which I later described as atomic blasts inside your head. That was an exaggeration, of course, and the most uncomfortable part of the procedure was the brightness of the light flashes during the photography.

After the operation, and it is called surgery, the doctor said that I could resume normal activity,...no restrictions. He said that I would pee yellow for a couple of days, and please don't call him about that because it is normal and harmless. I was given an Amsler Grid, a pocket size card with white vertical and horizontal lines on a black background and a white dot in the center. Holding the card about a foot away and looking at the dot with one eye at a time, the lines should appear straight. If they appear distorted, it's time to call the office for an appointment. I developed a habit of watching the lines at least once a day. The first time I looked at the card I immediately noticed a round black area in the upper left quarter of the card, a permanent hole in the macula, burned there by the laser.

Since I was concerned, to say the least, about the laser, I looked for and found diagrams of the eye to see if it would help me understand what was going on. My description of the structure of the eye, goes something like this. Imagine a soft ping-pong ball with a hole cut in one side and with that hole replaced by a lens, much like the lens in a camera. This lens is surrounded by a blue or brown circular ring, making the eye look the way it does when you look at someone's face. The ping-pong ball is filled with a transparent liquid under just enough pressure to keep the shape of the ball. The inside wall of the ball, opposite the lens, is covered with light sensitive cells. This surface is called the retina. A very small area in the center of the retina is called the macula. This is the place where my trouble begins.

When vision is normal and you look at something, light rays from the scene are collected by the lens and projected on the retina and macula. Wires and cable called the optic nerve, conduct the information into a wonderful computer in the brain and we see the scene.

Some of us are unfortunate enough to have unwanted blood vessels grow from the macula. Then sometimes they leak blood which kills the light sensitive cells and raises havoc with the scene. This is called exudative or "wet type" macular degeneration. The laser is used to seal the base of these blood vessels by burning them. Of course, the burning permanently destroys the cells at that location. Mysteriously the laser beam is able to harmlessly pass through the lens and fluid and be activated at just the right point. The control of such accuracy is unknown to me, but if I thought about the possibility that it might overshoot, I might really be nervous. But not to worry, you have to believe you're in the hands of an expert.

CHINA

I had always been fortunate to have doctors who were willing to answer my questions and this retinologist did it very well. So after the procedure and the follow-up I had many questions. Among them was one about travel. The leaking blood vessels in my eye made me wonder if flying and the changes in pressure might affect the condition.

We had traveled on a limited basis before retirement, but now had agreed that we would take the hard trips first, those being the longest flights to more challenging countries. Already booked was China in the fall of the following year, 1993, with a thirteen hour flight at over thirty-thousand feet on both ends. We had previously booked a flight and cruise to Alaska in the spring of 1993 and were thinking of more trips to Europe, India and Nepal for the future. When the retinologist heard the question he said I should take all the journeys. He didn't think that the flight and pressure changes would be of concern. He emphasized "go and enjoy." This seemed to fly in the face of saying previously that I should call immediately if I saw wiggly lines. I will always be grateful for his encouragement. I think he knew what a downhill ride I was on and that to miss these travel opportunities would be tragic. I remember justifying taking the chance that something might happen in my eyes, by thinking that I could leave a tour and fly home for treatment. So we went and had marvelous experiences. We saw Mount McKinley, Mount Fuji, the Great Wall, Terra-cotta soldiers, Hong Kong and so much more. We took hundreds of pictures and I began to give slide shows and lectures on our travels. My number of post-retirement hobbies was increasing.

The travel lectures came about when I told the program chairman of my Kiwanis Club that if one of his speakers could not come at the last minute, I might bring my slides of the trip I had made to the Soviet Union. It wasn't long before he called and I was on my way. At first I was only an emergency program, but soon I was asked to do all the trips as well as other slide shows I had put together. Then the local political club president wanted me to present a program. He was a great anti-Communist and thought I would strengthen his position with my slides about life in the USSR. It grew from there to a series each summer in the historic Methodist Camp-meeting village of Ocean Grove. This spurred appearances at senior centers around the area. It continued until I could no longer see the pictures.

What then was going on with my eyes? I wasn't worrying and perhaps I was in denial, although

I was still watching the Amsler Grid. It was not the grid that came as the first warning that all was not well. I began to notice that straight lines like door frames and traffic lanes had curves and hills in them. Then the grid showed distortions. It was back to the retina specialist for what was to become a familiar angiogram followed by the laser. This was the first time that I found that both eyes were involved. It was now nineteen ninety-seven and I was seventy-six. It had been five years since my disease was first diagnosed. I understand that some patients remain with one good eye which doesn't become involved. But I don't do things half way. This process was taking place over a couple of years, not months, and the retina doctor sent reports to the basic eye doctor for each procedure and he in turn continued to monitor my eyes. Then one day he found an increase in something called interocular pressure. Glaucoma! That was not good news, but although it is another eye disease without a known cause or cure, it is controllable in most cases by medication in the form of eye drops or surgery.

Glaucoma is another of the leading causes of blindness. The clear liquid which fills the inside of the eye, the pressure of which I think supports the shape of the eye, has a circulating system with the fluid flowing in and out. When the exit area becomes closed, the pressure increases. If left without treatment, it mashes the optic nerve at the back of the eye with naturally disastrous results. It is, therefor essential that the pressure be checked regularly by a qualified technician or ophthalmologist. You have no sense of the condition until vision is affected, and then it is often too late. Even if eye exams are not covered by insurance, eyesight is so precious that it's worth budgeting for these preventative exams. Often, particularly in senior citizen locations, eye screenings are done free. I did that once even while being treated for glaucoma and the test revealed a climb in pressure earlier than my next checkup!

Although the cause is unknown, the pressure can be controlled by medication, (eye drops) or if that doesn't work, a laser can punch a hole allowing freer flow of fluid, and if that fails, traditional eye surgery may be required. In any case, early detection is most important, and proper testing is the only way. I write this as a recollection of my experiences and research, and only with training as a mechanical engineer. My hope is that readers will be encouraged to seek proper professionals for the safety of their vision.

I did not realize at first that the eye drops, which are prescription medications, are systemic, that is to say that they enter your body by absorption through the eyes. Therefor it is important to tell other doctors what drops you are taking, just as any other medication. Doctors have books which can tell them of possible interactions between drugs, and some, or perhaps all pharmacies have computers which will automatically spot such interactions. I have learned to always disclose everything to every medical provider. It's a real safety measure.

I had never had anything but excellent vision, except for needing reading glasses after age sixty. I still had good vision. That is to say that what was not distorted was sharp and could not be improved by corrective glasses.

And then there are the cataracts. Nearly everyone I know, who has reached their late "70s or "80s have cataracts to some degree. A cataract is a disk already or hardening of the lens at the front of the eye. This of course interferes with the light rays which pass through the lens on their way to the rear of the eye. A cataract begins as a small area in the lens and grows slowly until sight is considerably impaired. An ophthalmologist should be seen regularly to track the growth and make a determination of the proper time that the cataract should be removed.

When my doctor told me that I had cataracts growing I did some research and found that in addition to a normal aging process, exposure to ultraviolet light is a prime cause. This corresponds to personal experience regarding a couple who are among our best friends. For many years they have owned boats on which they have spent much time, including weekends and week long trips during the summer months. Both of them have had cataract removal operations. The ultraviolet light coming from the sun is reflected on the water which means that it may come near doubling the rays that enter the eye. Ultraviolet light is also present on a cloudy day and it follows that it is wise to protect one's eyes from the sun's rays as much as possible, and beginning as early as possible in one's life. Spending time on the water, on the beach, or around a pool make one particularly susceptible. Activities such as golf, walking, or other time spent outdoors should be done wearing sunglasses. Buy sunglasses that are marked with the degree of protection they provide.

Treatment of cataracts has become nearly a routine surgery. New technology allows the cataract to be removed and the damaged lens is replaced with a plastic lens. Each lens is specifically made for the patient's needs so that the image will be correctly projected to the retina. Recovery time from this operation has become very short and any distortion due to swelling disappears within days.

In my research, I found some disagreement among experts about the relationship of cataracts and macular degeneration. Some information seems to indicate that a cataract operation may increase the onset of macular disease. Other experts say there is no such evidence. It is certain, however, as in my mother's case, a cataract operation will not result in improving vision that was lost to either macular degeneration or glaucoma. Now at age 82, I suffer from the triple header, macular degeneration, glaucoma, and cataracts.

Many years before, Del and I had taken some oil painting lessons and enjoyed them very much. Although I knew I would probably have more vision problems, I seemed to forget that and when in Florida for winter vacation, and looking for something to do, I took up watercolors. Learning color mixing, hues, tones, and values was very rewarding. It didn't hurt that the teacher was an attractive blond. I would progress with much practice to being able to paint neighbors homes in watercolor and have them hang them in their homes. Another hobby had been added to my list.

Speaking of hobbies, I had started collecting antique American clocks about twenty-five years before the eye problems began, and had learned to repair the clock movements. This was another hobby that incidentally required good eyesight. I was continuing to enjoy all my hobbies and life was good despite the overhanging threat of macular degeneration. Maybe it was denial, but I was reading all I could find about the disease. None of it, however, related to what I could expect in the ensuing month or maybe years.

Then one day the Amsler grid showed what might be a bad problem, now three years after the initial diagnosis. My other eye was now involved. I called at once and was given a priority appointment. This time it was called a blister on the retina. The trouble with this was that the usual fluorescein angiogram couldn't "see through" to spot the leaking blood vessel. But, not to worry, my retina man had a new "green machine" in his branch office, one of only two machines in the State. It is so called because of the dye color. The hidden vessels become visible to the camera with this dye. By now new digital cameras had replaced the old film process and many more images could be made which appeared instantly on the computer screen. They could also be saved on the computers hard drive and archived if desired.

It was during this period that a friend talked to one of the doctors from a prestigious eye hospital and arranged for me to go there for a second opinion. I told my retina doctor that I thought I would like to do that and he thought it a great idea and provided records for me to take. I think he realized that eye patients need to have this additional assurance that they are doing all that is possible. I am a great believer in second opinions, and an admirer of physicians who agree to it.

Actually, in my case, I found that my doctor, the New Jersey retinologist , had a better diagnosis than the hospital doctor had. Sometime during this process I learned that one of the important things the doctors were looking for in the pictures of the back of the eye, was "the hot spot". The hot spot showed up as a white dot and represented the source of blood entering the new growing vessel. This was apparently the target of the laser. The hot spot has a much longer technical name, which I neither remember nor care to remember. It was the hot spot having been hidden by the blister that required the green machine which could see through the blister wall.

The laser operation following the blister appearance, became the most scary of the treatments I had had. My vision was badly affected for a day or two. The entire area of my vision was clouded, objects were not clear, and riding in the car, I couldn't recognize buildings along the highway. I didn't know it then but this was a preview of the future.

I began to think of the consequences of blindness. There was no more denial after this. It was deadly serious from now on. The treatment was successful however, and after the post operative days, I was still able to see well enough to drive , paint, and take pictures. My usual life continued, but with some fears for the future. And our winter vacation of two or three months was coming up. We would leave for our winter home in Florida in January. It was now nineteen ninety-nine and I was seventy-eight.

FLORIDA

After having a serious eye setback, leaving for a new area a thousand miles away, I asked my doctor for recommendations in our vacation area. He had none but suggested that I look for a doctor with the "green machine". He would probably be most desirable. The trip to Florida that winter was uneventful with Del and me sharing the driving, two hours or fifty miles for each turn. When we arrived, and even before going to our condo, we stopped at the area hospital to see if they had a registry of retina specialists. They did not, but we found that the state of Florida had such a service and we were able to get the names of local doctors to call. The first did not have the machine, but a few calls later we found an outstanding doctor about an hour's drive from our place. We made an appointment to establish a relationship so that when we needed him he would be familiar with my case and it would save time.

This was the first time I had realized that retina specialists fell into classes of aggressive and passive when it came to treatment of wet type macular degeneration. The aggressive ones believe that the progression of the disease can be slowed by the laser treatments. Others seem to feel that little is gained, and both treatment and non-treatment come out the same. There is also some feeling that some doctors don't want to treat and take the flack for lack of results. Some patients opt for the passive approach for different reasons, and no one knows if they are right. I have been happy with the aggressive method and believe that I have benefited. The benefit was never that any sight was improved or restored, but that the rate of vision was slowed.

It is true that the laser does permanent harm and I was to see such damage in the next two years. It happened that the treatments became necessary while I was in Florida, and they resulted in noticeable vision changes.

During the first examination by my new Florida retinologist, he said to his assistant "he's got it in both eyes." And both eyes were leaking! So laser treatments were scheduled. When I got back to the condo, I called my New Jersey retinologist and asked if I should fly home. After hearing the story, he assured me that it would be more reasonable and just as safe to have it done in Florida. And so, another decision had been made. I had procedures done on both eyes.

After one session, for instance, objects were squeezed in the middle, or had only one end, like an automobile with only the back half visible. One day after such treatment, I was convinced that something had gone wrong, like my movement at the wrong time during the procedure. I called the doctor to make a further appointment and inquiry. I explained my concern to the nice and compassionate young lady on the phone, and she wished me a happy Valentine's Day. I remember hanging up the phone and shouting happy valentine and bursting into tears. Such is the journey with macular. She had also told me to come right in. After an examination, I was told that my condition resulted from swelling caused by the laser and in a few days the swelling would subside. And in the discussion that came afterward the doctor told me that five hundred thousand people in Florida were legally blind. When I repeated this to a friend later, he said that it was probably true and that all of them were driving.

It was true that in a few days the distortion caused by the operation disappeared. This swelling occurred in some, not all, of the laser operations I would have after this time, and would not upset me so much, especially the thoughts of a possible accident with the laser.

I was now really aware that I had better prepare myself for the future. With a really negative attitude, I decided to find a place where I might learn Braille. There was one not too far away from the condo so we went there to inquire. As so often happens in Florida, we talked with someone from our home town. After the seemingly necessary talk about home town news and mutual acquaintances, if any, we discussed Braille. He told us that his company worked mostly with blind children. What a sobering thought. And I had been feeling sorry for myself. After all, I had had a great life of over seventy years, including travelling the world, and these kids would not have that opportunity. He also felt that at my age a course in Braille would probably not be successful. He gave me some basic Braille lesson cards to try and I really couldn't distinguish the feel of various characters...I have never explored Braille again. The result of the visit was not to try to learn Braille, but he gave me a lead to a "magnifying" center. All of this proves the benefit of exploring the possibilities for help. The nearest showroom of vision aids was run by a nice gentleman, several years my junior, who told me that he was ninety percent blind from something called pigmentosa. The interior was dim because light affected his vision so much. This was my first introduction to closed circuit television readers. I really didn't need anything like that yet, but in addition to buying a hand-held magnifier, I happened to be there when a young lady from the main store came with a computer program which she proceeded to demonstrate. It magnified the computer screen up to sixteen times and could read items on the screen in a clear voice.

One of my very good fortunes was that I was computer literate, having used one in business. I was now using my third machine. After retirement I had taught myself touch typing with a computer program and could type thirty words a minute, error free. What a great tool that would turn out to be. I was given a free trial of thirty days, and bought the program thinking that the time to learn to use it was while I could still see. That was the way it worked out, although it would have been possible to learn it later.

This was about the time that I found that I needed more light to read and magnification of small print. I bought gooseneck lamps, halogen lamps, and magnifiers of various sizes. I found that the typical magnifying glasses sold in drug stores, and in flea markets, despite their labels are only about 2x magnification. That is to say they enlarge the image by two times. After using these magnifiers for less than a year, I found that they were no longer strong enough and the much more expensive 3x or 4x magnifiers like the one I bought at the vision aid store, was what I now needed. Even so, I found that large print books were all that I could read, at first directly and later with the magnifier.

It seems that as the macular degeneration progresses, so does the need to change vision aids. New technology and inventions continue to appear, and there is a big enough market so that they are readily available.

Florida seemed to be the place where the vision changes affected me most. One day I attended a meeting of our condominium association and sat next to a fellow from an adjacent building. We were chatting before the meeting started and when a sign-up sheet came around he asked me if I would sign his name because he could not see to do it. Of course I did, without asking questions. When the session ended we walked back to our units together and he told me that he had macular degeneration. It had come on about a year earlier and in six months he was legally blind. He had sold his golf clubs and his car. He and his wife now had to hire a driver to bring them to Florida. I saw him once the following year and then they stopped coming. I wondered if the doctor's statement that I was one of the lucky ones might have meant that my form of the disease was not fast acting. Since that time I have heard of other cases where blindness came very quickly.

One sunny afternoon I left the apartment to walk across the complex and realized that everything looked as if there were an eclipse of the sun. It was an amber half light and really depressing, especially after the bright colors seen in daily life in a Florida resort. On another day we were walking the beach by the ocean, and as I looked at the horizon, I remembered the sharp horizontal line between the sea and sky that I had seen in Maine. Now that straight line was broken by something that looked like mountains. I had no other indications of distortions at this time….. strange and troubling.

The nights became difficult because I couldn't sleep. I couldn't help thinking about the future and what it would be like. I kept a dim light on all night so that when I opened my eyes I could see something. I got up often and worked at the computer. Two of the products of this nocturnal activity were short one page pieces expressing my feelings about my eyesight. One was titled "On Losing Ones Eyesight". The other was called "Battle Plan" written apparently when my attitude was better. No one saw the former but I stuck the other on the wall to remind myself of positive thoughts. I found that it helped to write down my thoughts. Sometimes they were so negative that I would not save them and throwing them away seemed to dispose of the thoughts too.

Golf had not been much of an important part of my life although I had played for sixty years. In trying to continue doing as much as I could,

I played an occasional round with my wife and other couples at our par three course on the condo property. Of course someone had to watch the ball because I couldn't see where it went. One day, as golfers will appreciate, I felt that I had really hit a great shot. It really felt good. My caddie wife and the other couple oohed and aahed, and just as I was envisioning the ball landing right in front of the green, someone said "maybe you better hit another one". I asked where the ball went and was told that it was in the basement of a new building across a pond. It had been straight and long but in the wrong direction. I played very little after that.

NEW JERSEY

Home sweet home is an old familiar phrase. It was now beginning to be more meaningful each year. During the ten years between my seventieth and eightieth birthdays, in addition to fighting the macular degeneration, I continued to travel as my first retinologist had suggested. In addition to the annual trips to Maine and winters in Florida, we had several more trips to Europe and even a really big adventure in India and Nepal. But we knew upon return that there was no place like home.

I was beginning to find that life was easier if you knew where things were and you could maneuver confidently. That brings up driving.

Driving a car seems as natural to Americans as walking. It also represents personal freedom to most of us, so we naturally dread the time when we have to give it up. I, like most men, began driving as soon as allowed by law and had been sort of a car nut. I had owned many cars, some exotic, one of which was a nineteen sixty-one Mercedes 190sl. It had both soft and hard tops and was a joy to drive. As my vision failed, I kept trying to continue some "safe area" driving. Our home was riverfront, and if I stayed on the road around the river, there were no cross-streets. One day I saw a yellow line in the road and found that it was really a traffic pylon. It made quite a noise as I dragged it along. This little happening made me think that it was time to give the car up. I won't soon forget the night, a new years eve, when the car carrier came and took my sports-car away.

That should have been the end of my driving altogether, but I still took the family sedan out on the safe route along the river. I was suffering from light and contrast problems. Areas in bright sunlight were visible but those areas in shade were like night, and objects or people could not be seen. One day, as I reached a shady spot, a young woman pushing a baby carriage appeared right beside the car. I had not seen her at all. I drove back home, parked my car, and never drove again. I was lucky that I hadn't injured someone and, hard as it may have been, I hope that I would have stopped driving sooner.

What happened to our motor travel to Maine and Florida? As I related earlier, my super wife had always shared the driving. She, unlike some women, had a talent for operating an automobile and could drive stick shift or automatic shift equally as well. Fortunately, I was always at ease when she was at the wheel. Then my condition began to have its effect. I remember that on one sunny day I drove into the Baltimore Harbor Tunnel and suddenly realized that I couldn't see anything but the yellow line. Scary? You bet. The remedy was that the next time we came to any tunnel, and I was driving, I would pull over and let Del drive. This should have been a sign to quit, but we continued this way for a couple of more trips. Then I became a passenger only. And, we found, a rather useless one since I could no longer read a road map, or road signs. So, we stopped more often, drove fewer miles each day and learned to take our time and have a lot of patience. Macular degeneration has its effect on many more than its victims.

The end of the twentieth century was approaching and lots of things were happening. Major cities had count-down clocks, some in odd places like under water in Dublin and on the Eiffel Tower in Paris. Computers were expected to have trouble with the date change, and even the federal reserve distributed more cash to banks in case electronic transactions should fail. Nothing like that happened. But that was an upcoming milestone for me. I began the new century and millenium by learning that I was legally blind. I mentioned earlier the term Legally Blind. I wondered if I had reached that point. So I asked. Eye doctors seem to be reluctant to tell their patients that they have become legally blind. I had to ask. When my vision reached a point where I couldn't read, write or see anything below the big E and maybe one line below, I suspected I was there. The same was true with a friend who I prompted to ask. If you ask and the answer is that you are legally blind, ask the doctor to give you a note to that effect. They usually write it on a prescription blank and sign it. Sometimes an assistant does it, including the signature. This statement can be used to qualify for a federal income tax deduction and other benefits from the state and social security administration. In New Jersey the commission for the blind confirms the doctors statement and issues a letter on its letterhead certifying the patients eye condition.

This can be copied and used for various programs. It pays to ask about eye chart readings, pressure readings, and anything else you may think helpful.

What does legally blind mean? Because the federal government through the internal revenue service, allows a blind taxpayer a deduction from taxable income because of blindness, it is necessary to have a standard for determination of what is meant by blindness. Therefore Section 29-23Y of the Internal Revenue Law sets legal blindness as 20/200 (or less) vision in the better eye. These numbers come from the eye charts familiar to most of us, beginning in grade school and later in eye doctors offices. The card on the wall with the big E at the top. It is a way to compare the vision of an eye with the vision of a normal eye. If you can read the smallest print at the bottom, your eye and the normal eye can each see that line at 20 feet. Hence the term 20/20 vision. If however, your eye can make out only the big E, that is all you can see at 20 feet, while a normal eye can see it at 400 feet. This is 20/400. Very bad. So, legally blind is somewhere in the middle, but a good measurement of handicap or disability.

Having had regular eye chart tests in different doctors offices, I have noticed a variation in types of charts. The old white card is now rare because of the small offices size. The chart is now projected and bounced off mirrors, sometimes seeming less clear. The other light in the room may vary too. But overall, this seemingly simple test in a high tech world seems to be good enough.

In my case, in the future, I would be unable to see the big E, and the testers would have me count fingers that they held only two or three feet from my eyes.

When I began with Macular Degeneration, the internet was just becoming available to most of us. A year or so before becoming legally blind, I bought a new faster computer and was now able to "surf the net". Of course I looked up eye diseases and found a wealth of information. Some of the websites were started by sufferers, and were very informative and helpful. I learned more about the types of macular. The main ones are designated as dry and wet types. Eighty percent are dry and some wet type cases start as dry. The more I learned, however, I was convinced that these were two different diseases. There seems to be a couple of others which affect younger people. I have heard of no treatment for the dry type. It is caused by the accumulation of a yellow powdery substance called drusen on the macula. It usually is not so severe as the wet type. I think the wet type should have a name of its own. It is a little disconcerting to have people say, when hearing of your affliction, "Oh, my grandfather had that and he was still driving at ninety-five". The name also includes the term "age related", since mostly older people are stricken. Originally it was senile macular degeneration, but some kind soul felt that age-related sounded better.

In what I consider a frank discussion with my New Jersey retinologist I told him that I thought that laser therapy was equivalent to blood letting in revolutionary times. He thought that it was better than that. The discussion which followed was more positive about the future. He cited the advances in genetic studies and told me that if I would come back in twenty years he could cure me. I reminded him that I didn't have that much time, which of course he knew. It is also apparent that there is much more research since the population is aging and the disease is more common. New drugs are coming, and those being developed to counteract angio-genesis in oncology are promising.

Among the things I learned during my eye disease journey was an insight into the attitudes and concerns of the medical doctors. I found genuine compassion and concern in their explanations and treatments. Although modern medical offices are organized to make maximum use of aides and assistants, I noticed that the physicians were always right into my case and I never felt rushed or unable to ask them questions and discuss my feelings with them.

I became aware, after a time, that such statements as telling me to go ahead and travel, and telling assistants that I was out of there (no more appointments unless I might need them) made me feel more confident and less fearful of the future. One of the little things I picked up was after a discussion with my eye physician friend, as he rose from his stool he said softly, "too bad". I had a distinct feeling that he was in there with me. It must be difficult to manage the problems of malpractice insurance, patients with unreasonable expectations, office staffing and keeping up to date. I admired them and tried to be pleasant and cooperative even in the face of a disturbing ailment. I'm sure that it helped them help me.

I thought about the words, practice and patient. My meanings may not be the ones taught in medical school, but practice means to me that the learning is going on as one is being treated and knowledge of others being treated at the same time may assist in the treatment. And being a patient really means also being patient. The doctors on my team, as I like to call it, were most cooperative with one another, faxing information back and forth, and offering to be available to other doctors should I need to be treated away from my home area. I sensed a frustration among them that some of the diseases they have to treat are to some degree untreatable, or at least incurable. They often expressed their hopes for new discoveries leading to better quality of life for their patients.

On one of the Florida trips, I saw my Florida retinologist who monitored my glaucoma as well as the macula. After one check-up he asked if

I took any vitamin supplements. I had always avoided such things. He gave me the name of product which contained a variety of things thought to be good for the eyes. He said that there was no clinical evidence that the eyes benefited from these products but he had hundreds of older patients who claimed they were helped by taking them. My man back in New Jersey disagreed and said there was nothing to it. So, since there seemed to be no harm in taking them, I tried them for a couple of years. There was no noticeable effect, but just taking four large pills each day made me feel that, at least, I was doing something. My ophthalmologist, who I consider the leader of my team, and who seemed to keep up to date on such matters, said that there was some evidence that the dry type was retarded by such supplements. But, at the same time, any effect on wet type might be adverse.

The question of taking aspirin came up after an annual physical exam. Again, practicing medicine without a license, I asked if it would affect my wet type macular degeneration since it was an anti-coagulant. The physician said it was my call, so I didn't take it.

Then, shortly after arriving home from one of our Florida trips, another bomb burst. Heart Attack! It occurred at home, in the evening, complete with paramedics, ambulance, police and the emergency room. Despite the fuss, it was a minor attack, caused by a blockage in a secondary heart vessel. It was repaired with a stent and I was back home in three days. Then came the barrage of medication and cardiac rehab. Before long I began to think that all of this might have a negative effect on my eye disease. After consulting the cardiologist, retinologist, and ophthalmologist, I stopped all but one of the heart medications. That one had nothing to do with blood thinning or anti-coagulation. It was my decision. I have no idea whether it was right or wrong and I don't think the doctors know either. I do know that both eyes suffered more leakage in the six month period after the heart attack, than during any similar period since my original diagnosis.

I keep waiting for the bottom, wherever it may be. All the doctors say I will never be totally blind, and happily, nearly all victims do not reach that stage. Each doctor hedges a little by saying that only one or two of their patients has lost all sight. I have known others who have continued to have bleeding into their nineties.

I have learned much about the differences between the professions who treat eye problems. An ophthalmologist is a medical doctor who has studied the eye and specializes in eye treatment. Further specialization in parts of the eye results in practices limited to, for instance, diseases of the retina and vitreous. Then there is the optometrist. He or she has a degree which allows the use of the term doctor, although they are not physicians as the average person understands a physician.

They are basically skilled in providing corrective devices such as glasses. They do conduct eye exams, and can detect symptoms of disease, but are expected to direct the patient to competent professionals. Some ophthalmologists now refer to themselves as eye physicians, apparently to clarify the difference between terms. Some eye physicians now have optometrists associated with their offices, usually in a separate space, probably because it is a profitable venture for insurance and other matters.

The question always arises about the cost of a disease such as macular degeneration. It might have been a real burden for the elderly had not Medicare been legislated. Nearly all sufferers are elderly, retired and living on stable but moderate incomes. My experience has been that the typical macular laser treatment is approved by Medicare at about thirteen hundred dollars. Medicare pays eighty percent. If the patient carries a private Medicare supplement policy, the remaining twenty percent is paid by the supplement carrier (as well as the annual deductible).

A very important matter to me was being able to move quickly to get an appointment with the appropriate doctor, when something changed in my vision. Having to get approval, as required by some managed health plans, would have been unacceptable to me. One of my retina specialists posts a notice in his office that due to the nature of the disease he treats, it becomes necessary sometimes to see a patient without an appointment right away, and therefore other patients may be delayed. I heard little, if any, complaining about such delays. Most patients understood. So it follows that time required for insurance company, or prime provider approval is not in the patients best interest. Since I had a winter home over a thousand miles away from my usual medical providers, I found it important to be able to locate a professional and not have to worry about acceptance of my coverage.

Vision aids are another matter. They are not provided by Medicare, so such things as magnifiers, sunglasses, closed circuit television, and other helpful things are the responsibility of the patient. Most items are moderate in cost, but the CCTV (closed circuit TV) costs from about three hundred dollars to over three thousand dollars. Patients needing such equipment and unable to afford them should inquire of any groups for leads to sources of help.

I found that after I reached the point where a magnifier didn't help I had no need for an optometrist. I felt better off being monitored by my eye physicians and dealing with purveyors of low vision products like closed circuit television. Most of these provide for free trials, buy backs and trade-ins or consignment sales. There are also several sources of aids for the handicapped through catalogs and non-profit organizations. I have obtained several items from these sources at reasonable cost. I have a talking watch which tells me the time at the push of a button. It can be set, also, to announce the hour and I have mine set for the alarm, a rooster crowing, to sound at five PM, cocktail hour. Other items include a talking clock/thermometer, a talking calculator, and a "say when" which when hung over the rim of a glass buzzes when poured liquid nears the top. Even with this, I have learned to pour liquids over the sink. Missing a cup or a glass can make a mess on the table.

I was surprised to find that New Jersey has a state commission for the blind, which I am sure most, if not all, states have. It is a wonderful service for the visually handicapped, and trains and furnishes aids. Through them I was introduced to the state library for the blind, who provide Library of Congress Books on tape, free of charge. Even the postage is free. The commission even provided a letter to support my blind exemption on my income tax return. This may be the only bright spot in the whole thing.

The case workers from the Commission gave me several helpful things including a folding white cane and instructed me in its use. The cane is especially important at curbs and on stairs. Another advantage of carrying the cane, which I had not thought of, is that it is a sign to others of my handicap. I don't have to tell them that I can't see things or know who they are. It makes it easier for everyone.

JOURNEY'S END ??

What have I lost? What has happened to my quality of life? Too many things to enumerate. Let's start with the things I loved to do and with which I planned to fill my retirement years. Surprisingly, the most recently adopted hobby of watercolor painting seems to be the thing I miss the most. Perhaps that is because it was the most creative. I was not that good, but there are several friends who treasure and display the pictures that I painted of their homes. It is a most challenging hobby and one that requires continuing study. Gone also are photography and the illustrated travel lectures that I presented before local clubs and senior organizations. Over forty years I had collected and repaired antique clocks. That hobby has dissolved into finding someone to buy the collection. Woodworking and even gardening are impossible. Major travel is out, not that it is impossible but travel is really going to see something.

And of course there is driving, the freedom of movement so long enjoyed. Now I am wholly dependent on my dear wife and my old loyal friends to be able to go anywhere. I rarely ask to be taken anywhere and wait for offers, which sometimes I decline because I feel it might inconvenience the offerer. I am truly fortunate to have so many kind friends.

What can I do? Can I go to meetings, for instance? As my vision continued to fail I became reluctant to attend meetings and go out to eat with anyone other than my wife.

I had been a member of the Kiwanis Club of Asbury Park, New Jersey for fifty-five years. Kiwanis is an international organization of service clubs similar to Rotary International. Attending my club's weekly meetings at 12:15 each Thursday had been part of my life.

In two-thousand one, at a dinner-dance celebrating the eightieth birthday of the club, I was honored as "Kiwanian of the Year". I hoped it was not because I was their only blind member, and I was assured that it was because of my service to the club that qualified me. I was, incidentally, just three months younger than the club.

One of my long-time friends had been a member of the Club for fifty-six years, and we cooked up a little summary to impress new members. It went like this: Two of our members have belonged to the Asbury Park, New Jersey club for fifty-five and fifty-six years respectively, a total of one-hundred eleven years. They estimate that, between them, they have sung one verse of America, five thousand four hundred eighty-three times, driven twenty-one thousand nine hundred thirty miles to and from meetings, read two-thousand six hundred forty club bulletins, and eaten one thousand eight hundred twenty-seven chickens or parts thereof.

Also, paid six-thousand six hundred sixty dollars in dues. Total Kiwanis experience, Priceless! We had a lot of fun with that and it made the State Kiwanis news.

How could I ask fellow members to pick me up, take me to the meetings and help me sign in, and order lunch, I asked myself. I decided I could not do it. Then I found out that my oldest friend in the club kept calling to ask if I would go with him. My wife and he kept telling me I should go, so I tried it. I found that, not only could I do it, but everyone seemed to enjoy my being there and it made helping me a rewarding experience for them as well as me. Each meeting begins with the Pledge of Allegiance to the Flag, the singing of one verse of America (my country tis-of-thee), and a prayer. I could do all of these. When I first entered the room, however, I needed to pick out my name badge, sign in, read the lunch menu (at the door), and write my lunch choice. These I had no chance of doing on my own. I found that without my asking my friends picked up the menu and read it aloud. That, in fact, became a ritual with comments about the chef, and other humorous remarks. I tell them my choices and they write them down. I handle the money problem by handing the bills I'm carrying to the persons collecting, and telling them to take what they need and give the rest back. It's interesting to see the different ways people handle that. Some do it without a word, while others take special care to count out each bill and put it in my hand. The members I sit with let me sit facing away from the light of the window and bring me water and coffee, which is self-serve. They have come to know my preferences and get things for me without saying anything. I just say "thank you". For a while I wore a lapel pin that said "Please say your name", but by the time most people read it, it was too late. I cannot recognize people, except by the outline of their size and shape, or their voice. Most have gotten used to saying "Hi Roy, it's Bob", or whatever they are called. I went through periods of saying that I would give up going to the meetings, but thankfully, I continued. I feel so much better when I return home. I am still more a part of what is going on than I thought I could be.

The encouragement of my wife and friends is a necessity, however. The constant pressure of AMD can change your attitude quickly. Del and I like to dine out as often as we can, and I enjoy it very much. It also lets me practice eating. That may sound strange, but eating when you can't see presents some problems. Food has a tendency to slip off the edge of the plate onto the table and water glasses, or worse, Martini glasses are easily knocked over. After several apprehensive dinner dates, I developed confidence, and, I guess, the attitude that this is the way it is and if I am trying, I shouldn't worry.

The great source of strength is my wonderful partner Del. She deserves better than to have a blind husband, but never complains and is always positive. I know she suffers when I am down. She keeps telling me how lucky we are.

And then, there is depression. It is a sinister condition said to be common among those with low vision. Some doctors say that you can't lift yourself by your bootstraps and prescribe medication. I tried it but prefer to get along without it. Life remains like a roller coaster, good days and bad, even good hours and bad. Sometimes when I least expect it, when something goes wrong or I become frustrated, I may start to cry. It always seems to be just below the surface. That is pretty hard to accept for a man, but I know that it is more common than I thought among other men with serious handicaps. Come to think of it, no one ever told me that life would be easy.

How much can I see? I suppose most of my friends and family wonder. It's hard to tell them. I have had so many stages in the disease that were somewhat different, and it is possible that it varies from person to person. Now, basically, I see a full panorama, mostly colorless and diffused. In the later stages, darkness has fallen, especially inside. I can no longer see people and have to ask if they are in the room. Sometimes I may see their outline but when I look directly at them they disappear. The macula provides the central vision and most color perception, so when you try to concentrate on a visual subject, it just isn't there. Contrary to some thought, there is no black hole, although at mornings first light I can see a black area in each eye. I have been able to sketch these and take them to the retinologist who says they are valuable to him, and are part of my file. Apparently the eye compensates to some degree and the area blends into the fuzzy scene.

Some of the little things are the most annoying. Putting toothpaste on a brush, or an electric plug in a receptacle, are frustrating. Restaurant owners may feel that darkness is romantic or makes food taste better, but they sure don't think of us macular degenerates.

Life is reduced to doing what you can do, finding more things that are possible and trying to stay positive. I find that I get a lift from inquiring about others and not dwelling on my own misfortune. A neighbor who is a new widow and who has wet macular has been one who I could help, and doing so has been a great tonic. May future generations be freed of AMD.

I have been asked if I had looked at a scene with the idea in mind that it might be the last time I would see anything like it. I don't recall ever having that experience. I certainly did not think that way, although I was aware when I traveled that there would be a limit to the time during which I could see the beauties of nature. It would have been unnecessarily painful to think about every scene as if it would be the last time I would see it. I have become aware that the total sensation is much more than eyesight alone. For instance, If I were standing along the shore of the ocean looking at the sea the total effect would include a view in three dimensions together with the movement of the ocean, the sound of the waves, the feeling of heat on the sand, the coolness of the ocean breeze, and perhaps the smell of the sea, all of which work together in order to produce the sensation that we sometimes think of as sight. One day my wife's nephew was standing with me looking at the view across the river in front of our home. He remarked on how beautiful it was and I reminded him that I could not see it. I say that sometimes without thinking that I am embarrassing the other person. He was not embarrassed however and pointing to his head said that the scene was in my memory. How wrong he was. Even if my mind could recall the picture, it would be one-dimensional, still, and silent. There would be no feel of a possible breeze or any odors. I can remember what clouds looked like and what the ocean looked like but it is different from what I used to see.

I notice as time goes on, the ability to recall such detailed items as peoples faces decreases. I am sure that people with impaired hearing have the same feeling that part of a visual object is missing because they can't hear accompanying sounds. A simple test with a television set will give those with no impairments an idea of the result when either sight or hearing is missing. Just adjust the controls. Incidentally, many people complain about the quality of television programs and tell me that I am not missing much. Possibly so, but for a football fan it's pretty hard not to be able to see the game. I have had to go back to finding radio broadcasts of sports events and enjoying them the way I did when I was a boy. That's only one of the adjustments that have to be made.

There is also the matter of color. The macula seems to be the part of the eye that data is particularly important in rendering the sensation of color. I find that colors are no longer brilliant and indeed they can't even be identified. This turns out to be surprisingly important when dressing. For instance, it is impossible for me to tell the difference between gray slacks and brown slacks. I have taken to hanging my brown slacks on the same hanger with my brown jacket. Otherwise I wind up with unmatching outfits. I have already had occasion to go out with one black and one brown shoe. Things are not yet so bad that I have not been able to catch the fact that I had put on one black shoe and one white shoe.

And how do I dream? I remember that for most of my life my dreams were in black and white. I have no idea why though I might speculate that it was because in the early part of my life movies and photography were black and white. Early tests for television were in color and I could see color then so why didn't I dream that way too? I noticed in recent years that I would occasionally dream in color. When I remembered the dream in the morning I would remark to Del that I had a dream last night and it was in living color. And she would say congratulations. I still dream in black and white and sometimes color and occasionally my dreams include explaining to people in the dream that I am visually impaired. Figure that one out.

Do I ever think why me? No I don't, possibly because from the onset of the disease I was aware of the fact that my mother had suffered from macular degeneration also. I would guess that such questioning thoughts would only add to the mental pain that goes with visual impairment. I would also guess that others may gain some benefit from thinking that it is God's will. Although I rarely have heard sufferers of serious illnesses make that kind of statement, I'm sure that thinking it is God's will gains some benefit and helps people to bear their burdens. Also, it helps to say that it could be worse, and of course it could. Many things are worse but that does not alter the fact that when a person has an impairment it goes with him every hour of every day and it is not something that he or she can easily get away from. So it really doesn't help your friend much to say to him it could be worse. It's better just to say too bad or I'm sorry and go on to regular conversation.

My friends and family have been most supportive during the progression of my macular degeneration and during that time I observed varying conceptions of my condition. They range from thinking that I am totally blind to my being able to see or do things that I really can't. So as the recipient of their kindness, and to make them more at ease, I try to tell them what I can see and when I need help. I prefer not to be held by the arm. Del and I work well in close areas such as restaurants, with her hand behind her back and mine gripping her fingers lightly. I can follow in her footsteps without fear of bumping into a waiter and sending his tray full of dinners flying, which would be quite embarrassing. She also announces changes in our path, such as curb, high or low curb, all level, two steps up, etc. With anyone else I like best to follow them closely, and it is easier if their clothing contrasts with the surroundings. For instance, I can lose them from sight if they are dressed in white and going through a store with a white floor. Similarly, when Del wears a dark outfit and we enter a dark restaurant, I have trouble following her. The adjustment has to be mine. I really can't expect those who go out with me to dress in black and white stripes.

Generally, most macular patients are able to see objects without detail. For instance, I can't find our car in a parking lot. When I know which one it is I can find and open the door, get in and so on. So I don't need help, and don't really like it. I can see my dinner plate but not what is on it. So Del points out where on the plate the meat, potatoes and vegetables are located. Some of my closer friends ask if I would like them to butter my bread, which is one of those thing I find difficult. I am not at all embarrassed to say yes, thank you. Neither do I object to questions such as how are your eyes doing? I know friends are sincerely interested and I give as simple an update as I can, because no one wants to hear a medical history in answer to a simple inquiry. I want them to know my limitations, but I don't want sympathy, and I find that it works out just about that way.

What is it like to have a progressive disease? I'm sure that others who have diseases leading to serious disabilities or even death can tell more chilling stories, but no disease is more visible day by day and week by week. As the loss of vision progressed, particularly in the later stages, I could see the change. At first you can see the printed word less clearly, then only partially, then it seems too small, and finally you can see only white on black print.

Since the progression is pretty constant but not sudden, the most noticeable change is apparent when visiting a place where you have not been for a few weeks or months. The reaction is Wow!---I can't believe that I have lost so much sight. I noticed it particularly when moving from home to winter quarters and back. I remember particularly one incident while in Florida when I had been told that I needed another laser treatment and I was agonizing over the decision to go ahead with it. Del asked me if I wanted to go home to have the treatment. My reply was an emotional I don't want to go home again...ever! It is a shock to go home after losing another level of vision.

In addition to losing sharpness of objects and overall blurriness, the amount of light diminishes.

Ultimately I reached the point where I needed to keep lights on in the house on a sunny day to find my way around. The only way to know that the sun was shining was to see the bright spot on the floor. And speaking of sun, the glare of sun coming in a window renders other areas invisible. So my environment while inside is with shades down, lights on, even on a bright day. Depressing? Of course!

Outside I wear sunglasses at all times. I find that pale yellow lenses are best for me. They enhance contrast between objects and still allow enough light transmission to keep the scene from being too depressing. Wraparounds or side extensions help too in keeping sunlight from sneaking in from the side, and after all, we macular degenerates have only side vision left.

I have been told more than once by friends that they don't know how I cope with my affliction. It's true that it is always with you from the time you open your eyes in the morning until you go to sleep at night. But with time acceptance comes and if you try, you find things to do that are challenging and worthwhile.

The talking books of the Library of Congress give the opportunity to read a wide variety of topics. I chose not to be entertained only, but to use the opportunity to learn about history and the lives of famous people. And I find that very entertaining as well as a source of subjects of conversation in social settings. Learning more about music is in my future when I can find the time. I think the point is to not allow time to reflect on what your life could be like if you had normal sight. I really don't want to think about that.

I have no doubt that support groups are great. I haven't done that yet, but I have found out that my discussions with the one neighbor who has macular degeneration have allowed me to talk more in detail about how I feel than do discussions with my wife. Such talks only hurt her, and in turn hurt me. I feel better about talking but worse because she suffers for me, and that's unfair to her. It's enough of a burden to a loved one to have to care for a disabled spouse, without having to listen to recitations of his or her unhappiness. So, as the recovering alcoholics say, one day at a time.

EIGHTY-THIRD YEAR

The year between my eighty-second and eighty-third birthdays became significant. I mentioned that I suffered a heart attack which occurred two months before my eighty-second and the decisions I made about cardiac rehab and medication. My retinas continued to bleed. This was alternately referred to by the doctors as, oozing, leaking, bleeding, or hemorrhaging. When I questioned the terminology they said the terms were interchangeable. Whatever.

So that year, as fall approached, I was faced with another decision. Should I just wait it out or should I call the retina specialist? He said to call any time. When you are faced with loss of eyesight, you want to be sure you leave no stone unturned, and that you won't find yourself in the position of having someone say "Why didn't you call?" So I called, and it happened to be a time when the office was closed, so I left a message with the answering service. The next day was a Saturday and I received a call from the doctor. He told me that I had become a good judge of whether or not I had bleeding, and he would see me before his regular schedule Monday morning.

Del and I were there bright and early, and true to his promise we were first. After an examination with only a hand held light and head mounted magnifier, he confirmed that I did indeed have bleeding, but only in the right eye. At this stage of my disease, he said, he could not say that laser treatment would be effective. If I so desired, he would do it,...My call. I said, I guess I have nothing to lose, so why not. He offered to do it right then if I so desired. I didn't want to spend any more time agonizing about whether or not to go ahead so I opted to do it right then. I think that he used low power, but I'll never know. I'm sure that it was probably futile but it made me feel that I was doing something.

The thirty-day follow-up exam came and the eye was still "wet". By then, our trip to our winter home in Florida was near and we soon left for warmer weather. Arrival at our apartment in Florida was accompanied with the feeling I call "vision shock". It's the realization that you have lost so much sight since the last time you were in familiar surroundings. For the first month and a half, I still felt that the eye, and perhaps both eyes were leaking, and again decided to see my Florida retina specialist. His examination, done the same way as the doctor at home had done, was long and thorough with his taking many notes and making sketches on my chart. He said that both eyes were leaking blood onto the retina, and that he would do nothing, including making an angiogram. He didn't want to "stir the pot" as he put it. We had another frank discussion about the disease, and at the end, I asked him, "On a scale of one to ten, how serious is my case of macular degeneration?" His answer was "Nine point five, I've seen only one case worse".

That was an answer that was received with mixed feelings. I was, of course, dismayed that my case was so bad, but at the same time, I still had some vision. I could make my way around familiar surroundings, and at least see light and dark, and use, to a limited degree, the computer and the closed circuit television reader.

We continued our winter, and our usual dinner engagements with friends, although I found myself more and more inside with the blinds drawn. Bright sunlight was really a problem so I was much more comfortable inside, whether "reading" a book on tape, or writing on the computer. Here I was, fortunate enough to be able to winter in a warm climate, in a nice place, with great people, and I had to stay in a room with the light shut out. Should I be grateful for my good fortune, or should I resent my misfortune at having my disease? That may be the great question facing so many seniors. Each of us has to decide how we handle it.

My friend in Florida asked me the results of my visit to the doctor, and when I told him the story of the nine point five evaluation, he said " well, you're handling it well anyway". I was pleased that he felt that way, but little did he know of the internal turmoil I was experiencing.

In due time, the first of April, we left for home. Of course vision shock occurred again, not so much because of being unable to discern objects, but because of the lower level of light. That seemed to me to possibly be from some other disease or side effect.

I then had a scheduled appointment with my ophthalmologist team leader, who reviewed everything and told me that my optic nerve was OK and that he felt that my specialists were doing all that was possible. My glaucoma was under control, for whatever consolation that might give, as he said.

Then I had a pre-scheduled appointment with the retina specialist. And, good news, the eyes were both dry! This after a year of leaking. We had another "heart to heart" discussion, during which he told me of a new drug, which injected directly into the eye, had been found to stop the progression of the disease. This drug would not be available for another year and wasn't available outside the country either. He said that if it were available he would try it on me. Yet another lifeline with too short a rope. There had been so many that had come and gone. I followed up on several at universities on the east and west coasts, the coming of the photo-sensitive "cold" laser, and others. But the fact remains that AMD is still incurable, and for unexplained arresting, progressive.

Then, before I left, I asked, without mentioning my visit to the doctor in Florida, "on a scale of one to ten, how serious is my case?" Without any hesitation he said "Nine point five. I've had only two worse cases in all the years I've practiced." This should be reassuring to others who are undergoing the progression of AMD. My case is that bad and I am still seeing some things, enough to keep myself going.

During my eighty plus years, I have seen medical science, or perhaps more accurately, the art of medicine make great strides, which have resulted in extending life expectancy by many years. We have seen the development of vaccines for influenza, pneumonia and others, and heart surgery, and even treatment to minimize stroke damage. But while all these great things have happened, the folks who now live longer suffer from afflictions of the elderly, for which there are no cures. The result is a growing population of dependent people, some suffering hopelessly, that are burdens on society and their families. Macular degeneration may be one of the least of these diseases. Others include the terrible Alzheimers, and the even worse Lou Gherig's disease. Our generation seems caught up in a difficult spot. Hopefully, our leaders and our brilliant young people will be able to come together to achieve a more balanced result, one where a longer life may not have to be an undesirable one. How fortunate it was that in the nineteen sixties Medicare was enacted. Imagine the hardships and heartbreaking decisions that would have to be made if there were no medical coverage for the elderly.

With the extra time available as a result of not being able to do many things, thoughts of possible contributions to causing macular degeneration come to mind. Could it be, for instance, that one of the childhood diseases made a contribution? It seems to be agreed that genetic structures may be the cause, or just the weakened area which can be attacked by the disease. One definite harmful natural presence is ultra violet light, now thought to contribute to macular damage, as well as to the growth of cataracts. When I was about ten years of age, an eclipse of the sun took place. I can remember the day when a friend and I were playing in the back yard and it began to get dark. My mother came out and explained what was happening. She had with her a piece of glass and a candle. She held the glass over the candle flame until a smoky film covered the glass. Holding the blackened glass between the sun and our eyes, we could watch the passing of the moon across the face of the sun. We spent a considerable time doing that. We now know that it was a dangerous thing for our eyes. My mother was legally blind from wet macular degeneration for the last ten years of her life. My friend passed on before he would have been stricken so we don't know if all three of us would have suffered similar eye problems. In addition to that, I don't remember wearing sun glasses until at least high school, and then only rarely. And having been born and raised within a mile of the Atlantic Ocean beach, I spent more time on the sand and in water than the average child. Could that additional exposure have contributed?

When I was a youngster, I wouldn't eat spinach and other greens which now are considered important nutrients for eye health. Who knew about that at the time? Neither did I eat fish until later in my adult life.

It's too late for us now. But the sooner young people begin to live so as to limit their risks, the better chances they will have. And particularly since it seems certain that they may have life expectancies of a hundred or so years. Being ninety percent blind for the last twenty years of an extended life is not an attractive thought.

I spoke of my mother and her having macular degeneration. I think of her often now, and regret that I came so late to realize what she was going through in her days of declining sight. Fortunately, for both my mother and me, my business was only about two miles away from her home, and since a lot of my work was away from the office, I could stop often to see her and be sure she was alright. I knew that her sight was failing, but my father was alive and taking care of her, so I paid less attention to her disease than I should have. In the late nineteen seventies she had a cataract operation, and I remember how angry my dad was when it didn't improve her sight. I guess a lot less was known about macular degeneration then, but the doctor didn't explain thoroughly enough about any retina problem. Even so, she opted to have the other eye operated on and it too was not an improvement. The reason, of course, was that now the image came through the front of the eye to the retina which because of the macular degeneration, could not receive it. My mother and father were both devastated. As time passed, Dad suffered from dementia, not diagnosed as Alzheimers, and ultimately had to be cared for in a nursing home. I, an only child, now ran my mother's affairs, and maintained her home for her. This meant nearly daily visits and Sunday morning trips to the super market. At first we went together while she could see make out labels. Later she gave me lists, which I could hardly read, and I shopped alone, incidentally saving much time. I saw to it that she kept all doctors appointments, and followed up on vision aids which were not very plentiful then compared to the sophisticated products of today. Looking back I feel good that I was there for her, but I am sorry that I didn't know what she was suffering. As another friend of mine has said, you don't really know until you've been there yourself.

I can remember visiting mother on weekday afternoons and finding her seated on a straight chair in front of a television, watching a soap opera, with her face six inches from the screen. I know now that even that close she saw little.

I bought her lots of small portable radios, but unfortunately, I didn't hear about the books on tape. Even today it is unfortunate that such information is not more effectively provided by medical professionals and social workers. My advice for sufferers or their caregivers is ask lots of questions and follow up on all leads. There is more available to improve the life of the handicapped than you think.

As I approached my eighty-third birthday my days went something like this. Each morning when I awoke and opened my eyes, I was faced with a decision. That decision was whether to curse the darkness or to be thankful that I could see light outside the window. This decision might make the difference between having a good day or a bad one. All days now seem to fall into one of these two categories. Being still able to discern light carries through to being able, for instance, to make out the opening (door) to the bathroom, and once inside, to be able to identify the white blob in the corner as the toilet. Little things like that become very important to the visually handicapped.

In our living room, I have a recliner and a small table on each side. On the right is my tape player from the Library for the Blind, with headphones, on which I play tapes from the library. I refer to that as reading books, and in outside discussions I will say that I just finished reading so and so. It comes very naturally. Also on the right table is a Walkman with headphones, and pushbutton tuning set to favorite stations. On the left table, I have a portable tape player, modified to play the Library of Congress books on tape, but on this one I read the weekly news magazine supplied by the library. It to has its own headphones. And finally, on the left is an old portable radio tuned to my favorite station with good sound reproduction for music. Again, this unit has headphones. Why four sets of headphones? Close your eyes and try to insert the headphone jack into the small hole.

By the time you accomplish this you've missed a program or have ruined your day through frustration. I try to make everything as easy as possible. I'm still trying to organize my clothes so that I can find the ones I want. There are several types of tactile labels and pins available. My plan is to simplify by having fewer choices, and working from there. Like everything else, having things in the same place is essential. It is hard enough to find items when you know where they are. But if they get moved, we nearly sightless folks are sunk!

And so the sunset of our lives, for those of us with AMD, becomes a sunset as we've seen each day for all our lives. The objects of our everyday lives become less clear, and then less bright. In our case, sunset lasts all day, every day. But our lives still have beauty. But not the glorious reds, oranges, and purples, splashed across the western sky.

EPILOGUE

Research on Age-related macular degeneration continues and new treatments appear with increasing frequency. And as the population ages, so does the number of diagnosed sufferers. The long time favored laser treatment has given way to medications injected into the eye. The thought of that is more disturbing to me than the laser was. Not only that, but injections continue, in some cases monthly, for one or two years. Several manufacturers have products and, in the words of one of my doctors, they are hideously expensive. It also appears that they are not appropriate for everyone, since my doctor says that I am not a candidate for the treatment.

As these "golden years" pass, more of my friends of my age report wet AMD and tell me of their experiences with the new treatments. The process doesn't seem to bother them at all. The only unfortunate thing is that so many of them are disappointed because they don't recover lost vision. I have heard little, if any, claims of increased vision by doctors or manufacturers. The objective is to stop the progress of the disease. Only recently have I heard of a clinical trial combining an injection with a gene retarding drug. This is the first time I heard the term gene as a proposed therapy. Somewhere down that road, including stem cells, may lie the answer to sight preservation. Imagine the possibility of our children being able to receive a vaccine that would prevent AMD.

The road is long and the process complicated. Many of the large drug companies are reducing research and development. At the same time, maybe thousands of universities and small laboratories are patenting possible drug discoveries. They can't do the expensive clinical trials, manufacturing and distribution, so they sell their patented discoveries to the biggies. And the deep pocket companies are in less danger of patent infringement suits. When all is said and done, somehow we will find the answer.

All we want is a cure. But on the way we have to put up with Medicare part D, formularies, generics, doughnut holes, FDA approvals, Medicare approvals, insurance company rejections, and so on. Think of each step as the current miracle. And be positive. Encourage your doctor. He wants to keep you seeing as well and as long as possible.

Having now passed my eighty-sixth birthday, I find my life with low vision less troubling than the last few years. There are good days and bad days but downers are less frequent.

And for those beginning the journey, my retina specialist's experience is that eighty percent will stabilize after one occurrence, and of the twenty percent left, eighty percent will have only one more occurrence. That has proven true among my friends.

APPENDIX

ON LOSING ONE'S EYESIGHT

Disbelief, Anger, Grief, Resignation, Self Pity, Depression, Depression, Depression and more Depression. These are the feelings over which one seems to have little control. The anticipation of not seeing familiar things, especially the faces of those you love, are overwhelming. One hopes against hope that time will mitigate these feelings as it usually does. One problem is that sight loss is a constant reminder of itself, even when closing one's eyes at bedtime, the lights and weird figures are present. Loneliness can be easily added to the list.

Friends and family are sympathetic, but the sense that they are uncomfortable and don't know what to say is haunting. Keeping busy within one's limitations seems to help except for the constant inability to see normal things and perform simple acts. Frustration must be added to the list too. It is perhaps the most common feeling. The realization that sight is such an important part of life makes one feel that a substantial part of one's life has been lost. Certainly the quality of life is diminished to a major degree.

What to do? After the first month that major loss exists, the options begin to disappear, and reality and despair grow stronger. The only lifeline is the love and strength of one's spouse or other family members. Maybe time will heal but for the blind or partially blind, time is the enemy, not the friend.

Roy Garrabrant

TIME

Time seems to go more slowly now
And years seem slower too.
It's not that I'm just growing old
But so little I can do.
My paints, my brushes, my tools, my shop,
All of them are missing now.
I've known I've had to stop.
No more sports like football on TV
No magazines or books,
That's the way it will always be
For now that's how it looks.
And most of all I miss my ability to drive,
My dependency on others
Makes me feel I'm half alive.
The beauty of the sunsets,
The awesome starlit skies,
Are not as good in memory
As seen with your own eyes.
It seems to make no difference
What I try to do or how,
The fact remains, I'm sad to say
The days go by more slowly now.

Roy Garrabrant, Jr.

BATTLE PLAN

Keep in mind self pity helps no one.

I will keep cheerful for Del's sake.

I will leave nothing undone

which may help my problem.

I will explore all the aids I can find.

I will participate in everything I can.

I will dedicate my time to learning new things.

I will be grateful for my health and good fortune.

I will keep informed on events

and will participate as possible.

I will love those around me

for I am so lucky to have them.

One day at a time.

Roy Garrabrant

ABOUT THE AUTHOR

Leroy "Roy" Garrabrant has been retired for twenty years. He has a degree in mechanical engineering and after a short career in manufacturing spent forty years as an insurance and real estate broker. In addition to running his two office company, his speciality was appraising commercial, industrial, and residential properties. He served his community in several official capacities and as board member of charitable and business organizations. He had long time hobbies and travelled widely.

Shortly after retirement he was struck by wet macular degeneration and began a sixteen year gradual loss of vision. He wrote of his experiences during that period. He lives in Neptune City, New Jersey with his wife Della. They have been married over sixty years.

Printed in the United States
140665LV00002B/104/P